WINNING CLAIMS

VET RULES DECODED

SKIP GOODMAN

Copyright © 2024 Trient Press

All rights reserved. No portion of this publication may be reproduced, distributed, or transmitted in any form or by any means, including photocopying, recording, or other electronic or mechanical methods, without the prior written permission of the publisher. This restriction excludes brief quotations utilized in critical reviews and certain other noncommercial usages as permitted by copyright law. For permission inquiries, direct correspondence to the publisher, marked "Attention: Permissions Coordinator," at the following address:

Trient Press
5470 Kietzke Lane Suite 300 - #394
Reno, NV 89511

Criminal copyright infringement, including instances without financial gain, is subject to investigation by the FBI and incurs penalties of up to five years in federal imprisonment and a fine of $250,000.

Excepting the original narrative material authored by Skip Goodman, all songs, song titles, and lyrics cited within Vet Rules Decoded remain the exclusive property of their respective artists, songwriters, and copyright holders.

Ordering Information:
For quantity sales, Trient Press offers special discounts to corporations, associations, and other organizations. For detailed information, contact the publisher at the address provided above.
For orders by U.S. trade bookstores and wholesalers, please reach out to Trient Press at Tel: (775) 996-3844, or visit www.trientpress.com.
Printed in the United States of America
Publisher's Cataloging-in-Publication Data
Goodman, Skip
Winning claims : Vet Rules Decoded
Paperback: ISBN 979-8-88990-192-1
E-Book: 979-8-88990-193-8

TABLE OF CONTENT

Welcome..3

Acknowledgement... 4

Introduction..5

What is the Process/Understanding the Role of the US Department of Veteran Affair... 6

Classification/Character of a Discharge by the VA... 7

M21-1, Adjudication and Procedures Manual.. 10

Historical Interpretation of Law - Informal Claim Submissions Accepted............................ 14

Intent to File Requirements.. 15

Effective Dates/Protection Rules.. 18

What is Fully Develop Claims (FDC).. 20

Types of Claims for Entitlement to Service Connection... 23

Identifying the Claimed Issues.. 28

VA's Obligated Duty to Notify and Duty to Assist... 31

Appeals Modernization Act... 34

Regulations Veterans Need to Know Chart... 42

List of VA Forms..45

Veteran Resource List.. 47

WELCOME

T. S. & F. Consultant and Management, LLC is a veteran owned and operated business created in 2015 for the sole purpose to assist veterans in their struggle in filing for VA benefits claims without the red tape or the runarounds of the VA system. We provide the guidance to allow active-duty members and/or veteransthe option to either process their own claim without the confusion and be independent or fully use our services.

The fact of the matter is that the VA Disability Compensation claims process has been around since the endof the Revolutionary War – and NOBODY ever teaches Veterans nor active-duty members how to file a VA Claim properly with having to deal with added mental stress that can be discouraging.

The Founder, Tierell D. Goodman, is a 16-year combat (OIF) veteran that served in the US Air Force. He was medically retired due to suffering from combat related impairment. Without the assistance of a mentor, hewould have completely been lost going through the cycle of confusion in the VA Claims process. Upon studying and learning the process, he was able to develop a clearer path to a successful process to assist other brothers and sister at arms to avoid the pitfalls.

ACKNOWLEDGMENT

This book is dedicated to the people that saw more in me than I did myself while giving me the confidence that I lacked for so long. Without my support group of key family and true friends, I would not have bee
this. I thank you for everything that you all have done both spiritual and non-spiritual.

I like to thank first, God. I would be nothing without your grace and mercy. It was you that saved and pro me in Iraq. In that time and moment, I gave my vow to help others in need if it is your WILL not mine.
You have watched over me even when I thought you was not there but now, I realize that you have alwaysbeen there. I need to grow in the way you wanted me to grow to glorify you in all things.

Poppa and Momma Dear, thank you for the love you have shown and given me through the years as well as teaching me how good God is. I miss you so much and I have always remembered the life lesson you tauin always put God first in all I do (Deut 28: 1-15).

Mr. and Mrs. Howard, you have been a great mentor and supporter. Without you there would not be me and the ability to help reach more of our brothers and sisters at arms. I thank you for taking the time toteach and show me what it is I needed to know while being patient. Finally, thank you for all me to be par and have the ability to experience real family love. I love both of you so much. You are a blessing to me.

INTRODUCTION

It was once said that the meaning of craziness is doing things repeatedly and anticipating various outcomes. We don't know who said it, but it can be easily agreed that it is about as close to a "universal truth" as we can get. Subsequently, we can obviously concur that veterans fall in this class with regards to their VA Claims, as well. We, as veterans, keep on doing the same thing, throughout each year, and we expect the VAClaims Process to create an alternate outcome. We document similar structures. We employ similar agents -or utilize a similar free VSO. We send in similar papers, and we put forward similar cases. A similar sort of contemptibility happens constantly at the VA consistently, consistently, every age with no obvious difference in advancement. The VA Claims Process is intended to have the veterans to go through formality to deter the veteran from applying for their legitimately benefits without clear direction. It's gotten huge that even as the VBA battles to track down ways of lessening the build-up…. the requests overabundance is NOW developing to the mark of the quantity of years so that them might be able to hear a case has expanded. Time to roll out an improvement and quit rehashing what isn't working.

WHY HAVE I MADE THIS?

I designed this rule book to help guide many active-duty members and/or veterans who have been denied and confused with the process of the VA Claims. Those active-duty members and/or veterans have been leftwith being discourage and feeling beaten by the very system that vow to provide the assistance needed for serving this country. It was never meant for the system to be clear and concise on the steps to properly file aclaim with an understanding to why you need to file, how to file, etc. Now is the time to change the programming within the mind of so many veterans to make a stand and say, "No More." Many have forgotten that it is we VETERANS who have VOLUNTEER to protect the constitution of this country contrast to those that have not and will not volunteer nor will provide the very respect we deserve in protecting them when they will not and don't know how to protect themselves from foreign and domestic threats. It isus that have put our life on the line of death each day when are in and out of uniform to include our immediate families that suffer just as much as if they are on active duty serving. It is us that was given a promise to be taken care regarding impairments that have occurred while serving by the government. One would think veterans would be better taken care of without the long red tape nor the long myths that has been put out to the veteran community to keep confusion ongoing to discourage veterans from apply for what was rightfully agreed and expected fairly. The TIME is NOW to get what is OWE to ALL VETERANS regardless of political parties. It is not the political parties that is the issue the issue is the those in power (money) controlling the narrative but have not served and will not allow any of their own family members to serve to their privilege.

WHAT IS THE PROCESS?

The Veterans Claims Process can be muddled, and accordingly, numerous veterans don't acquire the advantages they procured. On the off chance that you served our nation as an individual from the US military, and we're hindered thus, either truly or mentally, your merit pays for your penance. If you feel overpowered or confounded by the cycle, you ought to consider working with an accomplished veteran's advantages lawyer, VSO, and accredited VA Claims Representative. The person can guarantee that you are following the veterans' cases cycle accurately to have a superior shot at getting your veterans' benefits supported. As a veteran of the U.S. Military, you might be qualified for specific veterans' advantages. These advantages could incorporate medical services, benefits, instruction, preparing, protection, work help, or lodging help. A few advantages help with progressing back to day-to-day existence, while different advantages give pay to an inability endured while serving your country. On the off chance that you trust youare qualified for these advantages, however, are not as of now getting them you should record a case.

Whatever the circumstance, try not to be hesitant to record a case for benefits you believe you merit.

UNDERSTANDING THE ROLE OF THE US DEPARTMENT OF VETERAN AFFAIRS (DVA)

For most, the veterans' cases interaction begins with the Department of Veterans

Affairs (VA).The VA plays two fundamental parts:

1. Giving clinical consideration to veterans, and
2. Paying benefits to veterans.

The veterans' benefits the VA handles include:

- Compensation for administration-related inabilities,
- Pensions to low pay, wartime veterans or their widows, and
- Compensation to widows and groups of veterans.

These responsibilities are divided between the Veterans Benefits Administration (VBA) and the VeteransHealth Administration (VHA). Since you are looking to process a claim for veterans' benefits (disability compensation or pension) you would be dealing solely with the VBA.

To begin, you need to guarantee that you qualify as a "veteran" as per the VA's definition: "an individual who served in the dynamic military, maritime or air administrations, and who was released or delivered under conditions other than disreputable." Know that regardless of whether you have a good release, the VAholds the option to decide if your handicap came from shocking assistance.

Classification/Character of a Discharge by the VA

The military's release characterizations are as per the following:

- Honorable Discharge/release (HD)
- Discharge under noteworthy (honorable) conditions (UHC) or general Discharge (GD)
- Discharge under other than noteworthy (Honorable) conditions (OTH) or unwanted release(UD)
- Bad Conduct Discharge (BCD)
- Dishonorable Discharge (DD) or excusal

Since the VA's language indicates that to be viewed as a veteran qualified for benefits, the release so much be "other than dishonorable," individuals with the initial three kinds of discharge/releases (HD, UHC, or GD) quite often qualify. Individuals with dishonorable releasesor discharges won't ever qualify.

It is recommended that veterans should apply to update their release situations with opening a case to decide advantage qualification, yet this includes one more extensive and convoluted VA guarantee measure.

Qualification Requirement for Benefits

To be qualified for VA handicap benefits, there are sure broad prerequisites you should demonstrate. To start with, you should show that you qualify as a qualified veteran under VA guidelines. Much of the time, in case you are a veteran and got a release under conditions other than dishonorable, then, at that point, you meet the VA's meaning of a qualified veteran. Whenever you have demonstrated that you qualify as a qualified veteran, you should then demonstrate that you have an inability that can be service connected. To have a disability that is identified as service-connected, you should show you have a current mental or actualhandicap that is essentially just about as probable as not identified with an in-serve occasion, disease, or injury. Then again, you can likewise get a disability service-connected that was brought about by an assistance service-connected disability.

What exactly is a claim?

As defined by 38 CFR 3.1(p):

"Claim means a written communication requesting a determination of entitlement or evidencing a belief inentitlement, to a specific benefit under the laws administered by the Department of Veterans Affairs submitted on an application form prescribed by the Secretary."

For the VA to have an actionable claim, the claim must be filed by a claimant.

A petitioner is somebody who has a likely privilege to VA benefits under the law. A respectably releasedVeteran is a petitioner. An individual, who has never served in the U. S. Military (or one of the other perceived qualifying gatherings) and is anything but a ward of a Veteran, can't be a petitioner.

In cases, as recently clarified, these people can be a candidate. Basically, any individual who knows how to finish up a structure can generally be a candidate, however just likely qualification to VA benefits under thelaw can make them a petitioner.

In this manner, VA has no commitment to settle the utilization of somebody who isn't a petitioner. VA willjust exhort them that they have no legitimate remaining to get VA benefits.

38 CFR 3.151 expects petitioners to finish and present a structure endorsed by the Secretary of the Department of Veterans Affairs (VA) when recording a unique case for handicap remuneration or potentiallyannuity.

Even more explicitly, for VA to acknowledge a proper case it should have adequate data on it for VA to recognize the petitioner, endeavor to check their status as a Veteran, distinguish an incapacity or advantagebeing asserted, and it MUST have the mark of the inquirer. Assuming that these things are not finished, the application isn't viewed as a proper case. It will be gotten back to the inquirer for finish of the necessary things.

Please be mindful of the significance of the time requirements for filing formal applications as outlinedbelow.

For original formal applications received before March 24, 2015, the correct prescribed

forms are:VA Form 21-526, Veteran's Application for Compensation and/or Pension
VA Form 21-526c, Pre-Discharge Compensation Claim
VA Form 21-526EZ, Application for Disability Compensation and Related Compensation
Benefits,VA Form 21-527EZ, Application for Pension

Standard Form Required for Recognition of Claim

Effective March 24, 2015, VA will only recognize compensation, pension, survivors, and related claims if theyare submitted on the required standard forms.
For complete claims received on or after March 24, 2015, the correct prescribed VA forms to use based onthe benefit sought are outlined in the table below:

If the benefit sought is ...	Then the prescribed form is VA Form ...
service connection (SC) (initial)	

increased evaluation, or a claim for a permanent and total (P&T) rating	21-526EZ
associated with a supplemental claim received within one year of the prior decision	20-0995, Decision Review Request: Supplemental Claim

VBA Regional Benefits Office Structure and Claims Processing Model

Each RO is managed by an overall Director oversight of RO limits, divisions, and activities. Divisions inside theRO join the Veterans Service Center and may in like manner fuse Loan Guaranty, and Vocational Rehabilitation and Employment, and give additional abilities to serve Veterans and their families interfacing with the different division and Veteran need. It is vital to observe that a few Loan Guaranty limits are together and that couple of out of every odd RO has commonly divisional limits in their different office. In any case, paying little mind to the detachment of explicit divisions inside a RO that may exist, the RO can regardless arrangement with your solicitations. The biggest division in every RO is the Veterans Service Center (VSC). This division handles all pay, and benefits claims from beginning receipt to a definitive choice. Annuity claims are handled by one of the three Pension Management Centers (PMCs) situated in Milwaukee,St. Paul, and Philadelphia ROs.

Training claims are dealt with in Regional Processing Offices (RPOs) situated in four areas around the nation:Atlanta, GA, Buffalo, NY, Muskogee, OK, and St. Louis, MO.

Every RO has the limit of managing public contact encounters for their area to help walk around clients. Allcalls are answered by VBA National Call Center representatives. The Pension Management Centers, Education Regional Processing Offices, Insurance Center, and Debt Collection Center have their own free solicitation phone numbers.

In numerous models, the RO will essentially manage all cases for the state where they are found. Regardless,with the introduction of the National Work Queue (NWQ), ROs will need to work Veterans' cases from wherever in the country. For those states with more than one office, obligations regarding different bits of the state are commonly parted between the working environments by geological cutoff points. In specific conditions, work will/can be moved beginning with one office then onto the close to be worked in view of legitimate requirements and close by RO claims taking care of cutoff points. All cases taken from candidates and submitted to VA will ultimately be given out to a RO with the supported capacity to settle the case.
Accepting the Veteran's cases record has been surrendered, the getting RO will request that it be madeavailable for access.

The CONSTITUTION of The UNITED STATES of AMERICA Established the CONGRESS which passes bills aboutVeterans which when signed into law by The PRESIDENT is codified as Title 38 United States Code (U.S.C.) which is interpreted by VA in 38 Code of Federal Regulations (C.F.R.) from which policy & procedural instructions are given in DIRECTIVES.

M21-1, Adjudication and Procedures Manual

The essential administrative direction that drives VA's exercises inside the Code of Federal Regulations is 38CFR Part 3, Adjudication and 38 CFR Part 4, Schedule for Rating Disabilities.

38 CFR Part 3, Adjudication, traces administrative direction that coordinates generally adjudicative exercises, strategies, and capacities performed by VA.

38 CFR Part 4, Schedule for Rating Disabilities, traces administrative direction that fills in as the structure for how administration associated handicaps for VA intentions are appraised and assessed.

The references in Part 3 of 38 CFR (Code of Federal Regulations) follows an intelligent mathematical arrangement from 38 CFR 3.1 through 38 CFR 3.2600. Also, in Part 4 of 38 CFR - the references follow intelligent mathematical grouping from 38 CFR 4.1 through 38 CFR 4.150

For instance, for Part 3, you should simply eliminate the "3" from the reference and you will see that all references are numbered from "1" through "2600." If you are searching for 38 CFR 3.203, you are looking for the 200 and-third guidelines in Part 3. 38 CFR 3.203 would then be found later 38 CFR 3.57 (the fifty seventh guideline) however before 38 CFR 3.557 (the 500 and fifty seventh guideline).

The Manual or M21-1 provides procedural guidance to Veterans Benefits Administration (VBA) and facilitates how VBA processes Veteran's cases. All things considered; the M21-1 was changed over from a manual with three appendixes to a seven-segment manual with three appendixes. As each succeeding part was conveyed, suitably named the Manual Rewrite (M21-R), the more prepared portions were revoked. At this point, the M21-1 has been divided into nine (9) Parts with relating subparts and content inside each Part separately.

Pay and Pension Service keeps up with the M21-1 procedural manual in an Information Mapping(r) style. Data Mapping(r) is a technique for introducing data plainly and succinctly. Moreover, Information Mapping(r) permits electronic clients to rapidly get to the latest and precise data. The Information Mapped M21-1 is housed on VA's inward Compensation and Pension Knowledge Management (CPKM) intranet site. Notwithstanding, you approach a similar data through the outside confronting Know VA Knowledge Base web webpage.

Moreover, material changes to the M21-1 are refreshed and reflected inside VBA "Changes by Date" area. Make certain to reference this part when regulation or guideline changes so you can check whether and how VA might have corrected specific important strategies.

Part I (Part 1) - Claimants Rights and Responsibilities Part III (Part 3) - General Claims Process
Part IV (Part 4) - Compensation Dependency and Indemnity Compensation (DIC), and Death Compensation Benefits
Part V (Part 5) - Pension and Parents Dependency and Indemnity Compensation (DIC) Part VI (Part 6) - Chapter 18 Benefits

Part VII (Part 7) - Burial Benefits
Part VIII (Part 8) - Accrued Benefits
Part IX (Part 9) - Ancillary and Special Benefits
Part X (Part 10) - Matching Programs

Part I (Part 1) - Claimants Rights and Responsibilities
This piece of the M21-1 frameworks procedural direction laying out the privileges and obligations thatClaimants save during the mediation interaction. The primary subjects of Part II include:

Chapter 1 - Duty to Assist
Chapter 2 - Due Process
Chapter 3 - Power of Attorney
Chapter 4 - Regional Office (RO) Hearings
Chapter 5 - Appeals

Part III (Part 3) - General Claims Process
This piece of the M21-1 blueprints procedural direction relating to the essential capacities and exercises performed by most of VBA workers all through the cases interaction. The central subjects of Part III include:

Subpart i - Overview of Claims Processing and Structure of the Veterans Service Center (VSC)
Subpart ii - Initial Screening and Determining Veteran Status
Subpart iii - General Development and Dependency Issues
Subpart iv - General Rating Process
Subpart v - General Authorization Issues and Claimant Notification
Subpart vi - Special Authorization Issues

Part IV (Part 4) - Compensation Dependency and Indemnity Compensation (DIC), and Death CompensationBenefits
This piece of the M21-1 diagrams procedural direction relating to support association handicap remuneration and passing pay advantages to incorporate turn of events, rating, and approval issues. Themain subpart subjects of Part IV include:

Subpart i - Claims Processing Improvement Model
Subpart ii - Compensation
Subpart iii - Dependency and Indemnity Compensation (DIC) and Death Compensation

Part V (Part 5) - Pension and Parents Dependency and Indemnity Compensation (DIC)
This piece of the M21-1 blueprints procedural direction relating to annuity advantages to incorporate turn ofevents, rating, and approval issues. The central subpart subjects of Part V include:

12

Subpart i - Eligibility and Development
Subpart ii - Rating
Subpart iii - Authorization issues

Subpart iv - Organization of the Pension Maintenance Centers

Part VI (Part 6) - Chapter 18 Benefits
This piece of the M21-1 layouts procedural direction relating to Chapter 18 advantages to incorporate turnof events, rating, and approval issues. The foremost section subjects of Part VI include:

Chapter 1 - General Chapter 18 Benefits
Information Chapter 2 - Spina Bifida and Other
Covered Birth Defects

Part VII (Part 7) - Burial Benefits
This part of the M21-1 outlines procedural guidance pertaining to burial benefits to include development,and rating and authorization issues and considerations. The principal chapter topics of Part VII include:

Chapter 1 - Burial Benefits and Allowance
Chapter 2 - Service Connected Death Burial
AllowanceChapter 3 - Transportation Allowance
Chapter 4 - Plot
Allowance Chapter 5 -
Memorialization
Chapter 6 - Exhibits

Part VIII (Part 8) - Accrued Benefits
This part of the M21-1 outlines procedural guidance pertaining to the handling of accrued benefits to include development, rating, and authorization issues. The principal chapter topics of Part VIII include:

Chapter 1. Eligibility
Chapter 2. Substitution in Case of Death of Claimant
Chapter 3. Development for Accrued and Requests for
SubstitutionChapter 4. Rating Accrued Claims
Chapter 5. Authorization and Notification

Part IX (Part 9) - Ancillary and Special Benefits
This part of the M21-1 outlines procedural guidance pertaining to ancillary and special benefits to includedevelopment, rating, and authorization issues. The principal subpart topics of Part IX include:

Subpart i - Ancillary
BenefitsSubpart ii -
Special Benefits

Part X (Part 10) - Matching Programs
This part of the M21-1 outlines procedural guidance pertaining to development and application of matchingprogram procedures. The principal chapter topics of Part X include:

M21-1, Part X, Chapter 01 - General Information on Matching Programs

M21-1, Part X, Chapter 02 - Social Security (SS) Verification Match

For additional information on the organization of the M21-1, refer to the KnowVA Knowledge Base hostedon the internet that provides more in-depth information on each of the parts of the M21-1.

As defined by 38 CFR 3.1(r):

"Date of receipt means the date on which a claim, information or evidence was received in the Department of Veterans Affairs..." In many cases the date the claim is received by VA is the beginning date of entitlementto a benefit. Therefore, it is imperative that if you take a claim from a claimant, you should get it into the VA's system as soon as possible. If you hold the claim in your office, you may adversely impact the date of receipt of claim by VA for the claimant.

Link to the manuals:
https://www.knowva.ebenefits.va.gov/system/templates/selfservice/va_ssnew/help/customer/locale/en- US/portal/554400000001018/topic/554400000004049/M21-1-Adjudication-Procedures-Manual

Historical Interpretation of Law - Informal Claim Submissions Accepted

For a communication or action received by VA prior to March 24, 2015, to have been accepted as an informal claim*, the historical version of 38 CFR 3.155 required claimants to identify the benefit(s) they wereseeking, such as compensation and/or pension.

If a claimant was attempting to reopen a previously denied claim or was seeking an increased disability rating, VA also required the claimant to describe the nature of the disability for which he/she was seekingbenefits. A claimant could accomplish this by identifying the body part or system that was disabled or by describing symptoms of the disability.

Informal claims were important prior to March 24, 2015, because VA could grant entitlement to benefits from as early as the date of receipt of an informal claim if VA received a formal claim within one year of thedate VA sent the claimant an application.

*VA only recognizes "informal" claims received prior to March 24, 2015.

Reference: For more information about the time limit for submitting a formal claim, see 38 U.S.C. 5102(c)(1).

Why Is This Important?

For your inspirations, having a fair cognizance of the past acts of VA's tolerating casual cases is significant. Inany case, considering that a casual case may be portrayed as a casual case whenever got by VA before March 24, 2015, you will likely not be dealing with any cases that will meet the guidelines of a casual case.

Current Interpretation of Law - Informal Claim Submissions No Longer Accepted

It is critical to take note of that VA quit enduring casual cases on March 24, 2015. Veterans/claimants needing the upside of filing an informal claim as indicated by generally acknowledged direction that shouldnow impart to VA an "expectation to document".

Inquirers might achieve this "aim to document" by:

Presenting a finished VA Form 21-0966, Intent to File a Claim for Compensation and additionally Pension, orSurvivors Pension or potentially DIC reaching a public call community (NCC) at 1-800-827-1000 or the National Pension Call Center (NPCC) at 1-877-294-6380 starting an application for benefits through:

- eBenefits/VONAPP Direct Connect (VDC)
- Stakeholder Enterprise Portal (SEP)
- Digits-to-Digits (D2D)
- contacting a Veterans Service Center (VSC)/Pension Management Center (PMC)

employee bytelephone or in person.

Intent to File Requirements

Three requirements must be met for VA to acknowledge a complete ITF:

- A complete ITF must identify the benefit sought. It must identify if a claim is Compensation orPension.
- The claim must be able to identify a claimant. Typically, this will be the Veterans C file number orSocial Security Number.
- The VA Form 21-0966 is signed by the claimant or authorized representative (VSO, VA Public ContactRepresentative, attorney, or agent if valid POA has been completed)

Note: ITF forms are now required to have a signature for all claims after March 24, 2015. The exception iselectronic claims. They are not required to have a signature.

Communication of Intent to File

A claimant's communication of an ITF is adequate for VA purposes if, in the communication, the claimant provides VA with enough information to identify the Veteran (and the claimant, if the claimant is not the Veteran) specifies the general benefit he/she is seeking (compensation and/or pension, or Survivors Pensionand/or Dependency and Indemnity Compensation (DIC)).

Notes:
The initiation of an application for benefits via eBenefits/VDC or SEP constitutes an acceptablecommunication of an ITF.

When an ITF is submitted in writing, it must be submitted on VA Form 21-0966. VA Form 21-0966 must besigned by:

- the claimant
- the claimant's Veterans service organization (VSO)
- a VA-recognized power of attorney (POA)

If VA can identify the claimant via information included on VA Form 21-0966 or other data submitted with the structure, the main areas of VA Form 21-0966 a petitioner should finish is the segments named GeneralBenefit Election and Declaration of Intent (Sections II and III on the July 2015 rendition of the structure).
Expect the claimants is the Veteran if he/she leaves the Claimant/Veteran Identification (Section I) of theform blank.

Note: Only one "intent to file" per general benefit can be active at any given time, and only one standardclaim form will correspond to the active "intent to file."

Communication Not Filed on the Prescribed Form on or After March 24, 2015

VA will consider a request for benefits which was not filed on an appropriate prescribed form on or afterMarch 24, 2015, as a request for application. As a result, VA will notify the claimant upon receipt of a request for application and request that the claimant submit a claim on the proper form.

VA will inform the claimant of:

- the appropriate form(s) needed to submit a complete application
- ways to submit their complete application
- the potential effective date if benefits are awarded, which will be the date VA receives theircomplete application

Why Is This Important?

For your purposes, having a good understanding of VA's current procedures for accepting a claimant's request for benefits and the necessary next actions is important. With this initial contact made by the claimant or on the claimant's behalf, VA will take necessary action to obtain a completed required standardapplication form to process the claimant's claim appropriately. If the required standard application is not received by VA this could potentially have an adverse impact on your client's claim or cause delay in processing claim altogether.

The communication of an ITF to VA is important because VA may grant entitlement to benefits from an effective date prior to the date of claim (DOC) if the claimant submits a complete claim within one year ofthe date VA received the ITF.

When the complete claim is received within one year of the ITF, the ITF is a DOC placeholder and other applicable effective date rules, such as 38 CFR 3.114 and 38 CFR 3.400, may be applied based on the date ofreceipt of the ITF.

Link to the ITF:

The Board of Veterans' Appeals (BVA) is a free body that concludes requests on questions with respect to all Veterans benefits. Individuals from the Board audit benefit claims conclusions made by nearby VA workplaces and issue choice on requests. These Law Judges, lawyers experienced in Veterans law and in checking on benefit claims, are the ones who can give Board choices. Staff lawyers, likewise, prepared in Veterans law, survey current realities of each allure and help the Board individuals. BVA is totally free from VBA and the Chairman of BVA reports just to the Secretary. BVA has purview of the allure on any ultimate choice on benefits made by the RO, and on any non-clinical choice made somewhere else in VA. The Board of Veterans' Appeals (BVA) is a free body that concludes requests on questions with respect to all Veterans benefits. Individuals from the Board survey benefit claims conclusions made by nearby VA workplaces and issue choice on requests. These Law Judges, lawyers experienced in Veterans law and in investigating benefitclaims, are the ones who can give Board choices. Staff lawyers, likewise, prepared in Veterans law, survey current realities of each allure and help the Board individuals. BVA is totally free from VBA and the Chairman of BVA reports just to the Secretary. BVA has locale of the allure on any conclusion on benefits made by theRO, and on any non-clinical choice made somewhere else in VA.

At the point when the allure cycle starts, the allure stays in the RO for the initial steps of the interaction, yetwhen the allure has been confirmed to BVA, the ward of the allure is moved to the BVA situated in Washington DC. Assuming you have a request on a case in redrafting status, call the RO that keeps up with ward over the allure until the allure has been affirmed to BVA. When an allure has been confirmed to BVA, you should contact BVA for any allure related asks from that point. We will talk about the investigative interaction in a different example.

The Court of Appeals for Veterans Claims (CAVC) is an autonomous body that isn't related with VA in any way. CAVC is a "Title II Court" with an extremely thin ward: it can take situations where a ultimate choice onbenefits has been made by BVA. When a case has been acknowledged by the CAVC, VA no longer has ward over the allure and admittance to the document is restricted to just those with appropriate approval. CAVC isn't organized to deal with phone requests regarding the singular status of cases and may not give admittance to unapproved people to help with giving solutions to any singular record requests.

A couple of administration associations give portrayal to CAVC, and surprisingly still this portrayal might berestricted to explicit cases CAVC might allow for portrayal and afterward even still for select reasons as dictated by CAVC. At the end of the day, even though the Veteran might need you to take his case to this degree of court, your association might decay to do as such. In those situations where the Veteran is determined, you ought to allude that person to a private lawyer who is approved to rehearse and address inquirers under the watchful eye of this court.

PURPOSE:

THE RATING SCHEDULE IS PRIMARILY A GUIDE IN THE EVALUATION OF DISABILITY RESULTING FROM ALL TYPES OF DISEASES AND INJURIES ENCOUNTERED AS A RESULT OF OR INCIDENT TO MILITARY SERVICE.

Effective Dates

Except as otherwise provided, the effective date of an evaluation and award of pension, compensation ordependency and indemnity compensation based on an original claim, a claim reopened after final disallowance, on claim for increase **will be the date of the receipt of the claim or the date entitlement arose, whichever is the later.** 38 CFR 3.400

Protection Rules

10 Years - Service Connection 38 CFR 3.957

Service connection for any disability or death granted or continued under title 38 U.S.C., **whichhas been in effect for 10 or more years will not be severed** except upon a showing that the original grant was based on fraud, or it is clearly shown from military records that the person concerned did not have the requisite service or character of discharge.

(Cannot be severed after 10 years but can be reduced)

20 Years - Evaluation of Disability 38 CFR 3.951

A disability that has been continuously rated at or above any evaluation of disability for 20 or more years for compensation purposes under laws administered by the Department of Veteran Affairs **will not bereduced to less than such evaluation** except upon a showing that such rating was based on fraud.

Disability due to VA Hospital Care or VA treatment

If it is determined that there is additional disability resulting from a disease or injury or aggravation of an existing disease or injury suffered because of hospitalization, medical, or surgical treatment, or examination,compensation will be payable for such additional disability. 38 CFR 3.361.

Paired Organs and Extremities

Compensation is payable for the combinations of service-connected and nonservice-connected disabilities, as if both disabilities were service-connected, provided the non-service-connected disability is not the result of the veteran's own willful misconduct. 38 CFR 3.383

- Impairment of vision in one eye because of service-connected disability and impairment of vision inthe other eye because of non-service-connected disability.
- Loss or loss of use of one kidney because of service-connected disability and involvement of theother kidney because of non-service-connected disability.

- Hearing impairment in one ear is compensable to a degree of 10 percent or more, service-connected, and hearing impairment (NSC) in the other ear, which meets the provisions of section 3.385 in the other ear.

- Loss or loss of use of one hand or one foot because of service-connected disability and involvement of the other hand or foot because of non-service-connected disability.

- Permanent service-connected disability of one lung, rated 50 percent or more disabling, in combination with a nonservice-connected disability of the other lung.

What is Fully Develop Claims (FDC)

As a rule, the case interaction starts when you apply, VA Form 21-526EZ. This structure can be found on our Veterans Forms Page on our site at [https://www.va.gov/find-forms/]. For the mostpart, an Intent to File, VA Form 21-0699 would need to be completed and submitted to the
VA. You can record your underlying case at your nearby VA office or clinical office, or you can document online through the VA at ebenefits.va.gov while the completed work on switching overto their new site [https://www.va.gov]. On the off chance that you feel like you need help submitting your claim, a delegate from the VA or from an assistance association can help you.
Once the structure is finished, the VA will start preparing your case.

VA created the FDC program giving veterans a way of acquiring good judgment, quicker. Cases submitted under the FDC program might be prepared by the VA within 30-60 days of accommodation. Successful cases filed being a unique case will bring about an additional year ofpay. FDC is a further endeavor by VA to assist in capacity pay asserts and decrease excess.

As an incapacitated veteran filing an FDC, you should expect the weight of gathering the vitaldocumentation and collecting and setting up your case with no assistance from the VA. Your waiver is your freedoms to the VA's typical "Duty to Assist" for your case.

The hypothesis is that on the grounds that your case is completely FDC – it is exhaustive and idealized – you are giving everything the VA needs to settle on an equitable decision. Besidesrequesting clinical tests and conceivable Federal records, all the VA needs to do is audit yourcase and make an assurance on it.

While this technique doesn't ensure an award of benefits, VA trusts the most optimized plan of attack, and for unique cases with extra benefits, are adequate impetuses for veterans to explorethe military personnel records framework and embrace the Veterans' claims all alone.

In principle, because the veteran does all the hard work without the VA's help, the veteran arrives at a quick and precise judgment. An impaired veteran might possibly have the capacity or strength expected to comprehend, find, and gather all essential proof all alone to really fostera triumphant claim.

On the off chance that the VA chooses your case isn't completely evolved (is deficient with regards to vital proof) the VA would remove your case from the FDC program, and the case would then go through the Standard processing measure.

Fully Developed Claims (FDC) are discretionary, and might be petitioned for

- Veteran's disability pay

- Survivor benefits

- Veterans benefits

To submit an FDC, VA encourages to electronically submit it at eBenefits.gov or va.gov. If you complete a paper FDC for VA handicap remuneration, you should finish VA Form 21-526EZ andvisit your nearby RO.

The VA designed the Fully Developed Claim (FDC) program for the purpose of:

- Reducing its backlog of pending claims
- Improving claims-processing timeliness

The FDC program allows VA to eliminate and diverts the time and resources it normally devotes to thetraditional claims process by requiring claimants that choose to participate in this program to:

- Submit their claim on a specific form that contains language which satisfies the notice requirementsof 38 U.S.C. 5103.
- Simultaneously submit all private medical treatment records with their claim
- Identify any relevant treatment records at a Federal facility
- Submit any additional forms or treatment records required under special circumstances that supporttheir specific claim

Only a claim filed on an EZ form is potentially eligible for processing in the FDC Program. If a claimant requests processing in the FDC Program but did not file their claim on an EZ form, or uses an outdatedversion of an EZ form, the claim will be excluded from the FDC Program.

Types of EZ Forms

- VA Form 21-526EZ - Application for Disability Compensation and Related Compensation Benefits
- VA Form 21P-527EZ - Application for Pension
- VA Form 21-534EZ - Application for DIC, Survivors Pension, and/or Accrued

BenefitsWe will discuss more about the FDC program in a separate lesson.

Discretionary Decisions and Claims for All Available Benefits

By law, VA is obligated to decide all claims placed before it. In live Veterans' claims, the law states that a claim for compensation may be accepted as a claim for Veterans Pension and vice versa. However, not allclaims for Veterans Pension are necessarily claims for compensation and vice versa. This type of consideration is called a discretionary decision.

For the VA to consider both benefits, there must be some indication that the Veteran is claiming both benefits. Consider the following criteria when deciding whether VA will make the discretionary decision to apply 38 CFR 3.151(a) in the context of the Standard Claims and Appeals Forms rule:

Regardless of which claims form is submitted, the information on the claim must constitute a substantially complete claim for the unclaimed benefit being considered under 38 CFR 3.151(a).
If VA Form 21P-527EZ is accepted as a claim for compensation, the claim form must include information that would otherwise be included on a claim for compensation.
If VA Form 21-526EZ is accepted as a claim for Veterans Pension, the claim form must include information that would otherwise be included on a claim for Veterans Pension including income information.

The evidence of record must establish a likelihood that the benefit will be granted.
The claim must be reasonably interpreted to reflect an intent to claim benefits for the issue at hand. Generally, this is reflected via the claimant listing the issue on the claim form.

Types of Claims for Entitlement to Service Connection

A Veteran may be granted entitlement to service connection in the following manners:
- Direct service connection
- Presumptive service connection
- Secondary service connection
- Service connection based on aggravation

Direct Service Connection

38 CFR 3.304 Direct Service Connection

Direct service connection (SC) means that a particular disease or injury was incurred in service. This is accomplished by affirmatively showing inception during service. There are three components to provingdirect SC. These are:

- Injury or disease that was incurred in service that is noted in service treatment records
- A current diagnosis
- Medical opinion (NEXUS) linking the current diagnosis to military service

All pertinent or relevant medical and lay evidence must be considered, including the service records (which may show the places, types, and circumstances of service and the official history of the organization in whichthe Veteran served.

38 CFR 3.310(c) Cardiovascular Disease

Ischemic heart disease or other cardiovascular disease developing in a veteran who has a **service-connected amputation of one lower extremity at or above the knee or service-connected amputations of both lower extremities at or above the ankles,** shall be held to bethe proximate result of the service-connected amputation or amputations.

38 CFR 3.310(d) (TBI) In a veteran who has a service-connected traumatic brain injury, the following shall be held to be the proximate result of the service-connected traumatic brain injury(TBI), in the absence of clear evidence to the contrary:

- Parkinsonism, including Parkinson's disease, following moderate or severe TBI;
- Unprovoked seizures following moderate or severe TBI;
- Dementias, if manifest within 15 years following moderate or severe TBI;
- Depression if manifest within 3 years of moderate or severe TBI, or within 12 months of mild TBI;
- Diseases of hormone deficiency that result from hypothalamus-pituitary changes if manifest within12 months of moderate or severe TBI.

Service-Connection for PTSD

PTSD is defined in the Diagnostic and Statistical Manual of Mental Disorders (DSM-5) as a trauma and stress-related disorder caused by exposure to a traumatic or stressful event (stressor).

It is not uncommon to include symptoms of anxiety, depression, fearfulness, externalizing angry or aggressive features, isolation, memory impairment, sleep impairment, and lack of interest in once enjoyed activities.

PTSD can be service connected as related to military service. There are currently 5 ways toestablish service connections for PTSD. 38 CFR 3.304(f)(1-5)

1. If the veteran was diagnosed while on active duty, the stressor is related to that service andhas a current diagnosis of PTSD.

2. If the veteran was engaged in combat with the enemy, the stressor is related to said combatand has a current diagnosis of PTSD.

- Combat with the enemy can be proven with combat awards, personnel records, and the DD214.

- If the veteran does not have a combat award, it can still be established if it is proven the veteran wasat the location of a combat event.

- If the combat cannot be verified, consider establishing it based on a statement of dear as discussedbelow.

3. If the veteran has a current diagnosis of PTSD, a statement of fear of hostile military or terrorist activity, and a VA or VA contracted psychiatrist or psychologist confirms the statement of fear is adequate to support a diagnosis of PTSD, to include its relationship to the statement offear.

- Fear of hostile military or terrorist activity includes being located within area endemic to those circumstances and was confronted with an event or circumstance that involved actual or threateneddeath or serious injury, or a threat to the physical integrity of the veteran or others.

4. If the veteran is a confirmed former Prisoner of War, the stressor is related that experienceand has a current diagnosis of PTSD.

5. If the veteran is claiming PTSD based on an in-service personal assault and the assault can becorroborated, has a diagnosis of PTSD and is related to the personal assault.

- This does not require verification of the assault, only corroboration.

- This includes any type of personal assault such as rape, sexual harassment, muggings, personal attacks.

- Corroboration can be obtained through lay statements, personnel records, treatment records, hospital records, police records, etc.

Military Sexual Trauma Claims

MST is a term used by VA to refer to a sexual assault or sexual harassment that occurred during military service. This includes women and men. A female service member is more likely to be raped than killed in combat.

More than 20% of females are sexually assaulted while serving their country. The military prosecutes less than 5% of the reported sexual assault cases.

According to DOD, 86.5% of sexual assaults are not reported, meaning that official documentation of many assaults may not exist. PTSD and other mental health conditions such as depression, anxiety, adjustment disorder, dissociative disorders, borderline personality disorder, and substance abuse are linked to MST.

Victims of MST may also have physical health problems like gastrointestinal symptoms, back pain, headaches, sexual dysfunction, or chronic fatigue. The VA provides free treatment for all conditions (physical and mental) related to MST. Even if a veteran is not eligible for VA healthcare, they can still be eligible for free treatment due to MST.

Due to the personal and sensitive nature of MST stressors, victims often do not report or document the event when it occurs due to shame, guilt, or fear of reprisal.

VA has specific regulations and procedures for MST claims that assist in developing evidence to support these claims. Regulations with special liberalizing considerations for claims for PTSD based on MST are found in 38 CFR Section 3.304(f)(5).

Presumptive Service Connection

Presumptive service connection is considered when diseases or conditions are considered to have been incurred in or aggravated by service if manifested to a compensable level within the time frame specified for that certain disease under the regulation as outlined in the table below, even if there is no evidence of such disease during service.

Type of Disease or Condition Regulation for Presumption of SC chronic disease 38 CFR 3.309(a) disease associated with service of the following categories:

- Tropical Diseases
- Former Prisoner of War (FPOW)

- exposure to ionizing radiation,
- exposure to certain herbicide agents (currently, boots on ground or brown water service), or
- exposure to contaminated water at Camp Lejeune.
- 38 CFR 3.309(b)-(f)
- diseases based on full-body exposure to mustard gas or Lewisite.38 CFR 3.316
- diseases associated with service in the Southwest Asia theater of operations including:
- undiagnosed illnesses
- medically unexplained chronic multi-symptom illnesses
- Compensation for certain disabilities occurring in Persian Gulf veterans. (Undiagnosed Illnesses andInfectious Diseases)
- Diseases associated with service in Afghanistan 38 CFR 3.317(c)(2)
- Presumptive service connection for amyotrophic lateral sclerosis for all veterans (ALS or Lou Gehrig'sDisease). 38 CFR 3.318
- Non-Hodgkin's Lymphoma is a presumptive for Blue Water Navy, 38 CFR 3.313

Secondary Service-Connected Disabilities

38 CFR 3.310 Disabilities that are proximately due to, or aggravated by, service-connected disease or injury. It is not necessary to prove that the secondary condition was incurred or presumed tohave been incurred during service or aggravated by service. It is necessary to prove that there is a causal relationship between the primary and secondary conditions.

- Have a Service-Connected (SC) Disability
- Current Diagnosis (Condition)
- A medical opinion linking the current diagnosis to the service-connected disability.

For more information, refer to 38 CFR 3.310.

Aggravation of Preservice Disability

38 CFR 3.306 A preexisting injury or disease will be **considered to have been aggravated by active military, naval, or air service, where there is an increase in disability** during such service,unless there is a specific finding that the increase in disability is due to the natural progress of the disease.

Just because an injury or disease worsened during military service, does not mean that it shouldbe service connected.

It must show that the increase in disability was not due to the natural progression of the disease.

Service connection based on aggravation means there is an increase in severity of a particular non-serviceconnected (NSC) disease or injury that is attributable to aggravation by a service-connected disability, andnot to the natural progression of the NSC disability. The NSC injury or disease may have existed prior to entering active duty or after military separation.

Proper analysis of the evidence for presumption of soundness is very important to making a determinationof aggravation.

VA will carefully analyze the evidence for aggravation of a claimed disability when:
- under 38 U.S.C. 1153, a condition for which the Veteran is seeking SC was noted at entry
- under 38 U.S.C. 1111, a condition for which the Veteran is seeking SC was not noted at entry, butevidence proves that the condition pre-existed service

Keys to Service Connection

New and Relevant 38 CFR 3.2501

- Evidence not previously part of the actual record before agency adjudicators.
- Is information that tends to prove or disprove a matter at issue in a claim.

Medical Opinions

- Review of private medical and service treatments records must be mentioned
- NEXUS or LINK. (Medical opinion)
- Rationale on how the opinion is justified

Time Frames

- Within 1 year New and Material evidence can be used for readjudication
- After one year the claim will be considered "claim to reopen"
- Effective dates (Dates of claim to reopen)

BASIC REQUIREMENTS:

1. Confirmed exposure to whatever presumptive that the veteran is filing exposure to:

- VA will confirm the exposure through the veterans Service Personnel Records and through theBranch of Service.

2. Confirmed diagnosis of a presumptive condition that is on the presumptive list for thatspecific exposure.

Identifying the Claimed Issues

What is an issue?

A single claim can have multiple issues. Each item listed on a claim is a separate issue. All claims processingdepends on identifying the issue(s) being raised. Correct identification of the issues upfront allows for appropriate development and actions and outcomes when the claim is being adjudicated and all is said anddone.

For example: The Veteran is explaining to you that he has just returned from Iraq. While there, shrapnel from a land mine wounded him in both legs and abdomen. He has obvious facial disfigurement. He asks if the VA can help him enter a job-training program, since he has not been able to find work. He has made noprevious claim with VA.

Remember that a claim is defined as "a written communication requesting a determination of entitlement orevidencing a belief in entitlement, to a specific benefit under the laws administered by the Department of Veterans Affairs submitted on an application form prescribed by the Secretary."

An issue on the other hand, can be defined as an expressed or inferred request for a consideration by VA fora benefit. VA can consider this issue as a request for benefit consideration on the claimant's behalf.

Responding to issue requests that may arise can be as simple as your providing information on a topic or ascomplicated as your assisting in proving an injury occurred in service and is related to a current disability.

VA is obligated to address all claims and issues made by the claimant, but in addition, VA will also address any other benefits the claimant could be entitled to whether he or she has specifically claimed them or not.

Issues can be related or unrelated to the specific claim being made. Let's take a closer look at some of theseclassifications--expressly, reasonably raised, unclaimed subordinate and ancillary issues.

Expressly Claimed Issues

An expressly claimed issue is defined as when a disability and the benefit sought are both explicitly identifiedon a standardized VA form.

For Example, let's say that epilepsy is listed as a claimed disability on VA Form 21-

526EZ.Result: The issue of epilepsy has been identified as the issue seeking

consideration.

Reasonably Raised Claims

A reasonably raised claim is a claim that is not explicitly identified by the claimant on a standardized form but is identified upon review of the claims folder during the decision-making process for an expressly claimed issue. A reasonably raised claim arises based on a sympathetic reading of the claimant's statementsand/or evidence of record. It encompasses such things as entitlement to any ancillary benefits that arise because of the adjudication decision additional benefits for complications of an expressly claimed condition.

For example, let's say the Veteran's VA examination shows that his service-connected (SC) posttraumatic stress disorder (PTSD) warrants an increase to a 70-percent evaluation at the examination. In addition, the Veteran reported that he has been fired from several jobs due to his inability to deal with stress, and the VAexaminer identified the Veteran's stress management problem as a symptom of his PTSD.

Result: The decision maker addresses the issue of PTSD as it was the expressed claim and the reasonableraised claim of individual unemployability (IU) in the rating decision.

For instance, lets' say the Veteran submits a claim for SC for right knee strain. The evidence of record, including the resulting examination, shows that SC for the knee strain is warranted. The examination also reveals a knee scar that resulted from a post-service arthroscopy procedure. The examination indicates thearthroscopy was associated with the SC right knee strain. The examination also shows that the scar is not painful or unstable and is less than 6 square inches.

Result: If the examination is otherwise sufficient for rating purposes, the decision maker awards SC for the knee condition and separate SC for the no compensable knee scar as within the scope of the claim for SC forright knee strain.

Unclaimed Subordinate Issues

Unclaimed subordinate issues are issues derived from the consideration or outcome of related issues.Often, the primary and subordinate issues share the same fact pattern

For example: SC for treatment purposes under 38 U.S.C. 1702 based on a denial of SC for compensationpurposes is considered a subordinate issue:

- for a psychosis based on wartime service
- for any mental disorder based on Gulf War service
- when entitlement is shown under 38 U.S.C. 1702

Ancillary Benefits at Issue

Ancillary benefits are secondary benefits that are considered when evaluating claims for:

- compensation
- pension
- Dependency and Indemnity Compensation (DIC) entitlement

Note: Eligibility for ancillary benefits is derived from a Veteran's entitlement to disability benefits or thecircumstances of the Veteran's death.

For example: The Veteran is granted a 100-percent evaluation or amyotrophic lateral sclerosis (ALS) and complications, and the VA examination shows that he requires the daily assistance of his wife to attend to hisactivities of daily living.

Result: The Rating Veterans Service Representative (RVSR) addresses the issues of aid and attendance (A&A),Chapter 35--Dependents' Educational Assistance (DEA), specially adapted housing (SAH), and automobile allowance and adaptive equipment in the rating decision.

The Service Officer's Role in the Claims Recognition and Issue Identification Process

Given the seemingly involved processes that VA undertakes when adjudicating claims, you as a claimant's VSO play an important role in ensuring that your client accurately completes and submits the proper application for entitlement to VA benefits. If the incorrect procedures for filing the claimant's claim are followed or information is missing, it could result in the delay of processing of your client's claim. Therefore,whenever the intent of the claimant is unclear, and/or the benefit sought is not clearly identified, ask the claimant to clarify the issue to ensure appropriate development and accurate decisions. Inform the claimantthat VA will take no action pending clarification of intent.

You should always be acting in your claimant's best interest. Similarly, in doing so, you should always strive to ensure your claimant's submitted claim for entitlement to VA benefits captures what he or she is intending to claim. Remember that VA must decide on all issues that the claimant raises, so if your claimantdesires VA to consider certain issues, it must be clearly specified in the claim.

VA's Obligated Duty to Notify and Duty to Assist

VA must effectively notify the claimant of information necessary to substantiate his or her claim. Additionally, VA has a duty to assist claimants in gathering the evidence necessary to decide their claim, andmust consider all evidence gathered, for and against the claimant, in reaching their decision.

Duty to Notify

Under 38 U.S.C. 5103, VA must provide notice to the claimant of any information and medical or lay evidence not previously provided that is necessary to substantiate the claim. VA has traditionally referred tothe required notice in 38 U.S.C. 5103 as a VCAA Notice. However, because of amendments to the law since the Veterans Claims Assistance Act (VCAA) of 2000, the term Section 5103 notice has now replaced VCAA Notice, and you will see this term used throughout the manual and all relevant VA correspondence.

Similarly, upon receipt of an incomplete application for benefits or an intent to file a claim or apply for abenefit, under 38 U.S.C. 5102, VA must also:

notify the claimant of the information necessary to complete the applicationdefer assistance until the claimant submits the information

How is Section 5103 Notification Obligation Met?

VA has historically provided claimants the required Section 5103 notice in a paper-based letter after receiptof a substantially complete application for benefits. However, an amendment to the law has afforded VA more flexibility in how and when VA delivers the notice. Currently, most Section 5103 obligation is met through VA's providing this notice on the actual claims applications themselves.

Section 5103 notice is provided to claimants:

on a standard EZ application form when filing:
- a claim through the Fully Developed Claim (FDC) program
- a claim through the standard claims process

through online claims submission via:
- eBenefits
- the Stakeholder Enterprise Portal (SEP)

When an automated Section 5103 notice is generated during the establishment of the claim via:
- Veterans Benefits Management System (VBMS)
- Letter Creator

In rare instances, Regional Benefits Offices (ROs) may still need to send claimants the traditional Section5103 notice letter but only when one of the above methods was not utilized in the filing of the claim.

Duty to Assist

Under 38 U.S.C. 5103, VA must make reasonable efforts to assist a claimant in obtaining evidence necessaryto substantiate a claim. This assistance includes obtaining relevant federal records, relevant private records adequately identified by the claimant, and a medical examination, if necessary to decide the claim.

Substantially Complete Application

Under the provisions of 38 U.S.C. 5103, VA's duty to assist claimants begins when a "substantially completeapplication" is received. This is defined in 38 CFR 3.159(a)(3) and includes:

- the claimant's name
- his or her relationship to the Veteran, if applicable
- sufficient service information for VA to verify the claimed service, if applicable
- the benefit claimed and any medical condition(s) on which it is based
- the claimant's signature
- a statement of income in claims for Veterans Pension or Survivors Pension and Parents' DIC

If the application is not "substantially complete," as previously explained, under 38 U.S.C. 5102, VA must notify the claimant of the information necessary to complete the application and defer its assistance untilthe claimant submits the necessary information.

Once VA has received an adequate application, its duty to assist begins. Specifically, VA has an obligation to:

- notify claimants of the information or evidence that is necessary to substantiate their claim
- assist claimants that file a substantially complete claim in obtaining evidence to substantiate theclaim before VA decides on it
- make every effort to request all the evidence it needs to decide a claim based on the recordsavailable when the claim is filed
- undertake development to obtain additional evidence as it is identified by the claimant and/orhis/her representative make reasonable efforts to obtain:

records held by a Federal records custodian, such as:
- Service Treatment Records (STRs)
- treatment records from a VA facility
- Social Security Administration (SSA) records
- request completion of VA examination to support claim if required
- records identified as being in the possession of other Federal records custodians
- privately held records the claimant identifies, if the claimant provides the proper authorization forrelease of the records to VA

* Grant every benefit supported by law, which is consistent with the facts of the case, while protecting the interests of the government.

In its duty to assist with obtaining private treatment records or other private records identified by the claimant, VA will make no less than two attempts to obtain these records. Additionally, VA will notify the claimant of its efforts as well as encourage him or her to submit relevant private medical records if such submission is not burdensome.

In most cases VA will allow for 30 days for these records to be obtained (first attempt provides 15 days for response; second attempt provides 15 days to respond). If the records do not reach VA within 15 days after the second attempt to obtain them, VA will decide the claim without them.

VA will do everything within its power to assist the claimant in substantiating his or her claim. However, claimants are ultimately responsible for providing VA with evidence to substantiate their claim.

The provisions of 38 CFR 3.159 provide those claimants must cooperate fully with VA's reasonable efforts to obtain relevant records from Federal and non-Federal evidence custodians.

Specifically, for non-federal records the claimant must provide enough information to identify and locate the existing records, including the person, company, agency, or other custodian holding the records; the approximate time frame covered by the records; and, in the case of medical treatment records, the condition for which treatment was provided.

For federal records, if requested by VA, the claimant must provide enough information to identify and locate the existing records, including the custodian or agency holding the records: the approximate time frame covered by the records; and, in the case of medical treatment records, the condition for which treatment was provided. In the case of records requested to corroborate a claimed stressful event in service, the claimant must provide information sufficient for the records custodian to conduct a search of the corroborative records.

If necessary, the claimant must authorize the release of existing records in a form acceptable to the person, company, agency, or other custodian holding the records. This authorization usually means that a release form that is Health Information Portability and Accountability Act (HIPAA) compliant must be completed and furnished for evidence requests. VA Form 21-4142, General Release for Medical Provider Information to the Department of Veterans Affairs (VA), is HIPAA compliant and will allow VA to request private medical records on the claimant's behalf.

You can help your clients and help expedite the decision-making process by:

- Keeping the latest version of VA Form 21-4142 on hand

- Having the claimant complete the form upon the initial submission of his or her claim

Appeals Modernization Act

New Decision review Process

Here are the three lanes from which a claimant may choose in seeking review of a decision.

- Supplemental Claim -an opportunity to present a new claim with additional evidence that is new andrelevant.

- Higher-Level Review. - An entirely new review of the same evidence by a high-level claim'sadjudicator in VBA. You can't submit any additional evidence in this lane.

- BVA Appeal - Notice of Disagreement will be reviewed by a Veterans Law Judge at the Board ofVeterans Appeals (BVA).

Board Dockets

Below are the Board Dockets which will allow three separate dockets for handling the followingcategories of appeals:

- Appeals where the claimant requests Board review on the same evidence that was before the VARegional Office (VARO).

- Appeals with no request for a hearing but where the claimant elects to submit other forms ofevidence.

- Appeals where the claimant has requested a hearing.

It's important to note, two lanes are local VA Regional Office options commonly referred to as local lanes or VBA lanes. Work in either of the local lanes will be assigned through the NationalWork Queue. The third lane, the BVA lane is worked directly by the BVA in D.C.

It is **only recommended** to request a hearing. For this reason, the claimant can conduct a videohearing of a judge while presenting his or her cause for their case of an increase, reverse a denial, etc.

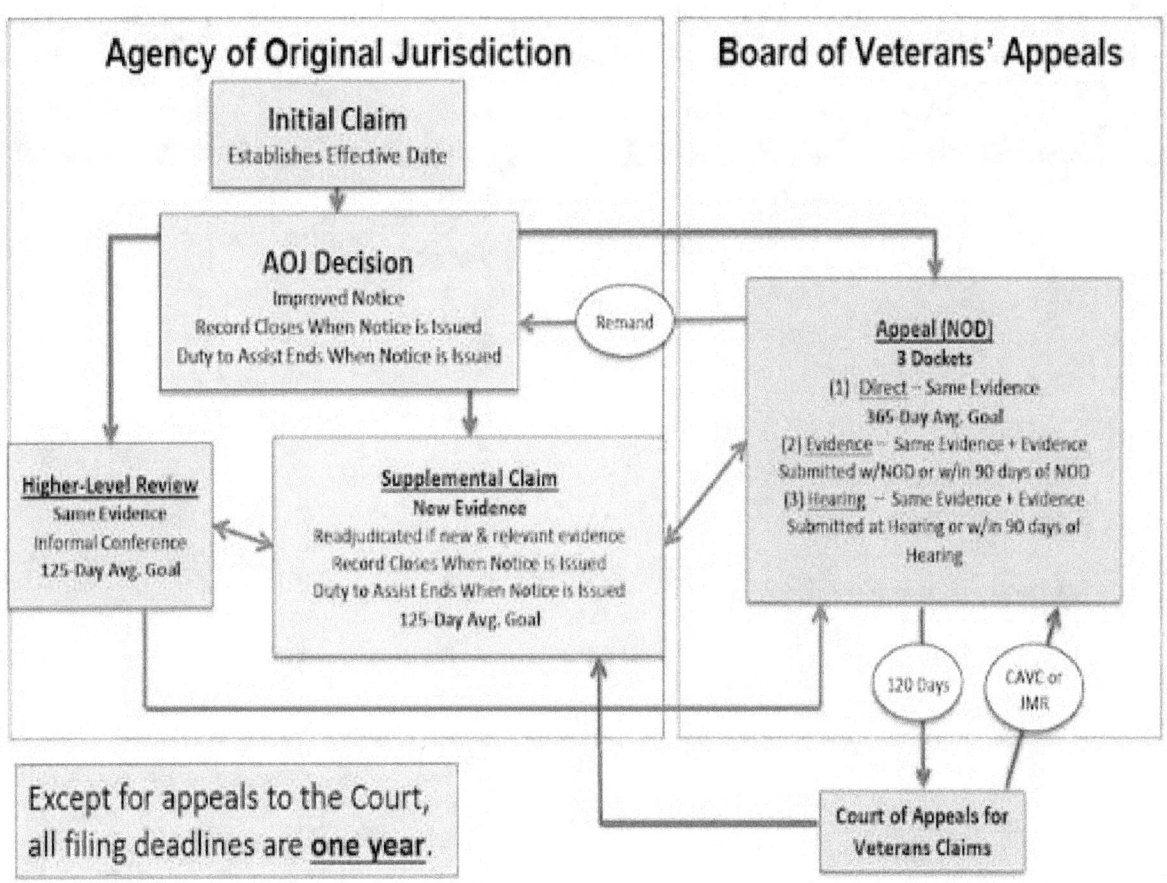

Which Board docket to choose?

	Direct	Evidence	Hearing
When to choose	If you think a **mistake** was made.	If you have **new evidence** you want a Judge to consider.	If you want a **hearing** before a Judge.
What will happen	The Judge will review the same record and make a decision. **No new evidence** will be added.	You will have **90 days** from your NOD to submit any new evidence. The Judge will make a decision considering the evidence you provided.	You will be placed on a list for a hearing before a Judge by videoconference (or in DC). After your hearing you will have **90 days** to submit new evidence. The Judge will make decision considering the hearing and the evidence you provided.
How long	**365 days** (on average)	**Over** 365 days	Based on availability. Currently the Board has 98 Judges. There are 69,500 Veterans waiting for hearings.

Supplemental Claim

Claimants may request a review of VA's decision by submitting a supplemental claim after a decision by the VBA, the Board, or. the Court of Appeals for Veterans Claims.

The definition of "supplemental claim" is "a claim for benefits under laws administered by the Secretary filed by a claimant who had previously filed a claim for the same or similar benefits on the same or similar basis." The VA is required to rededicate the claim if new and relevant
evidence is presented or secured with respect to a supplemental claim.

A supplemental claim is a request by an appellant to have their claim/appeal(s) reviewed by VBA based on **additional evidence that is new and relevant** to the benefit(s) sought.

A supplemental claim must be filed on the appropriate application form with new and relevant evidence, or the veteran must identify new or relevant evidence that VA can assist in gathering, to be complete the application.

New evidence means evidence **not previously submitted** to agency adjudicators, and relevant evidence means evidence that **tends to prove or disprove a matter** in issue in a claim.

VA will not decide a claim with incomplete applications.

A claimant is required to file a supplemental claim on a form prescribed by the Secretary and that the **duty to assist** in gathering new and relevant evidence will be triggered upon the filing of a substantially complete application.

Claimants should obtain all new and relevant evidence, and then prove it with a completed **VA Form 20-0995, Decision review Request: Supplemental Claim.**

A substantially complete supplemental claim application must identify or include potentially new evidence. An incomplete claim will be considered filed on the date of receipt if the complete application is filed within a year.

The intent to file does not apply to supplemental claims

Higher-level Review

A higher-level review (HLR) will consist of a de novo review of the issues **based solely on the same evidence** that was before the initial adjudicator. The higher-level review is conducted by a different more experienced VA employee with the ability to change the initial decision based on difference of opinion authority, subject to the rule that favorable findings are binding absent clear and convincing evidence to the contrary.

The higher-level review provides the opportunity for resolution of the issue(s) in dispute at VA without having to file an appeal to the Board or having to submit a supplemental claim with new and relevant evidence.

An HLR consists of:

- More experienced VA employee takes a second look at the same evidence (closed record and no duty to assist).

- De novo review with a full difference of opinion authority.

- Duty to assist errors returned to lower level for correction (quality feedback)

- A claimant is required to file a Higher-Level Review on a form prescribed by the Secretary.

- Claimants must complete a **VA Form 20-0996, Decision Review Request: Higher-Level Review.**

- The intent to file would **not** apply for Higher-Level Review.

Claimants *don't have the option of presenting new and relevant evidence* outside of a supplemental claim, and the two instances in the BVA lanes. Thus, if any evidence is received outside of those instances, it
will *not* be considered or acted upon in any way.

New Process – VBA Lanes

Supplemental Claim Lane

- VA will readjudicate a claim if "new and relevant" evidence is presented or identified with a supplemental claim (**open record**)
- VA will assist in gathering new and relevant evidence (**duty to assist**).
- Effective date for benefits always protected (submitted within 1 year of decision)
- Replaces "reopening" claims with "new and material" evidence

Higher-Level Review Lane

- More experienced VA employee takes a second look at the same evidence (**closed record and no duty to assist**)
- Option for a one-time telephonic **informal conference** with the higher-level reviewer to discuss the error in the prior decision
- *De novo* review with full difference of opinion authority
- Duty to assist errors returned to lower-level for correction (**quality feedback**)

	Supplemental Claim	Higher Level Review
When to choose	If your claim needs **new evidence**.	If you don't need new evidence, but think a **mistake** was made.
What will happen	**VA will help** you gather the evidence. A new decision will be made looking at the new evidence.	A **higher-trained** VBA employee will review your claim and make a new decision. **No new evidence** will be added.
How long	**125 days** (on average)	**125 days** (on average)

BVA Appeal Lanes

Once a decision is rendered by VA, and a Notice of Disagreement is filed, the appellant has three distinct lanes within BVA lanes to choose from. Each particular lane will have its own docket.

Direct Review - receives direct review by the Board of the evidence that was before VA in the decision on appeal. The Board has **365-days** timeliness goal for this docket.

Evidence Only Review Lane - must submit evidence within the 90-day window following submission of the NOD. The Board does **not have a duty to assist**, and the **record is closed.**

Hearing Lane - will be scheduled for a Board hearing. Additionally, the appellant may submit evidence within the **90-day** window following the schedule to hear. The Board does **not have a duty to assist**, and the **record is closed.**

A claimant is required to file an Appeal on a form prescribed by the Secretary.

Claimants must complete a **VA Form 10182, Decision Review Request: Board Appeal (Notice of**

Disagreement).

The intent office would **not** apply to BVA appeal.

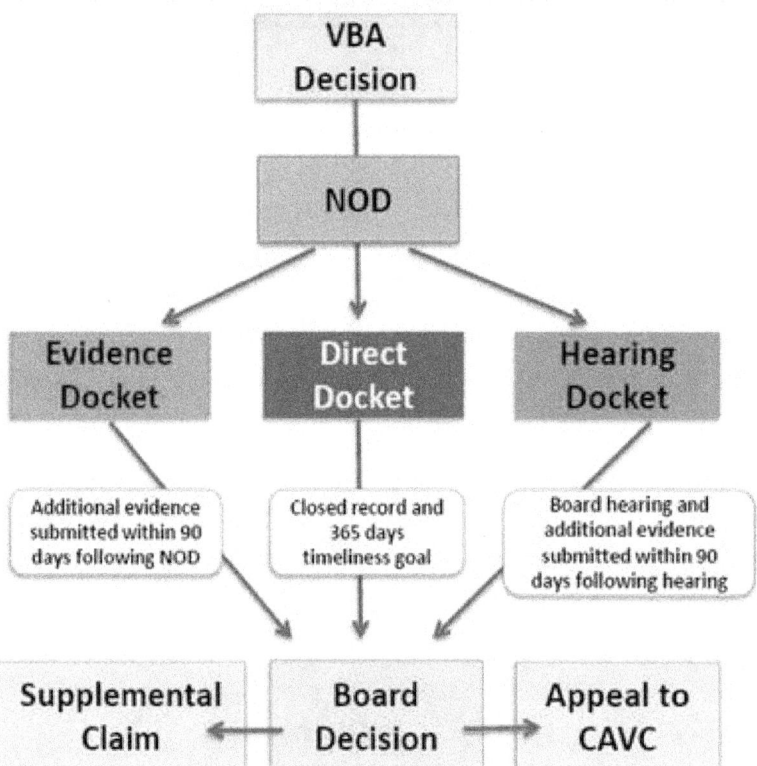

Regulations for Veterans to Know

38 CFR Part 3

Regulations	Section	Title	Notes
38 CFR Part 3	3.102	Reasonable Doubt	
38 CFR Part 3	3.105 (a)	Clear and Unmistakable Error	
38 CFR Part 3	3.155	Informal Claims	VA is to process informal claims automatically constrast to formal claim
38 CFR Part 3	3.156	New and Material Evidence	
38 CFR Part 3	3.304	Direct Service Connection; Wartime and Peacetime	
38 CFR Part 3	3.305	Direct Service Connection; Peacetime Service before January 1, 1947	
38 CFR Part 3	3.307	Presumptive Service Connection for Chronic, Tropical, or POW related disease, or Disease associated with exposure to certain herbicide agents; wartime and service on or after January 1947	Expose to Agent Orange
38 CFR Part 3	3.327 (b)2	Re-Examination	No medical examination if condition has not improved in 5 years
38 CFR Part 3	3.34	Total and Permanent Total Ratings and Unemployability	
38 CFR Part 3	3.35	Special Monthly Compensation Ratings	
38 CFR Part 3	3.352	Criteria for Determining Need for Aid and Attendance and "Permanently Bedridden"	
38 CFR Part 3	3.75	Entitlement to Concurrent Reciept of Military retired Pay and Disability Compensation	20+ years of service to get retirement pay and disability pay
38 CFR Part 3	3.804	Special Allowance Under 38 U.S.C.	
38 CFR Part 3	3.807	Dependents' Educational Assistance; Certification	Education assistance for dependence based on veteran at 100% or IU
38 CFR Part 3	3.809	Specially Adapted Housing Under 38 U.S.C. 801 (a)	
38 CFR Part 3	3.809a	Special Home Adaption Grants Under 38 U.S.C. 801 (b)	
38 CFR Part 3	3.81	Clothing Allowance	Applying for clothing allowance refer to

38 CFR Part 4

Regulations	Section	Title	Notes
38 CFR Part 4	4.3	Resolution of Reasonable Doubt	Refer back to 3.102; Must be in favor od the claimit if there is a doubt.
38 CFR Part 4	4.6	Evaluation of Evidence	How the VA evaluatemedical evidence
38 CFR Part 4	4.7	Higher of Two Evaluation	
38 CFR Part 4	4.14	Avoidance of Pyramiding	
38 CFR Part 4	4.15	Total Disability Rating	Define total disability and permanenet disability

Reference	Section	Title	Description
38 CFR Part 4	4.16(a)	Total Disability Ratings for Compensation based on Unemployability of the Individual	determine total and permanent disability based on individual and/or combine rating
38 CFR Part 4	4.16(b)	Total Disability Ratings for Compensation based on Unemployability of the Individual	Unable to obtain a substantial gainful occupation determine by SSA
38 CFR Part 4	4.18	Unemployability	Unable to obtain a substantial gainful occupation determine by SSA and medical reason
38 CFR Part 4	4.26	Bilateral Factor	Calculation for two extremities of opposite side of the body
38 CFR Part 4	4.27	Use of Diagnostic Code Numbers	Identify the impairment based on the 4-digit numbers
VA Manuals			
M21-1MR	Part III, Subpart IV, 2, B.7.j		Information on the approval of rating decisions prepared
M21	1 III,II,2,Sectin C(2)	Informal Claims Received Prior to March 25, 2015 Communication of an Inent to File (ITF), and Requests for an Application	Claim to be process by the VA upon receiving military medical records from serving branch
M21	1MR III, I, 2 Secion D	Integrated Disability Evaluation System (IDES)	Being Process with MEB
M21-1MR	III, ii, 2 Section G & F	Requests for Reconsideration	Reconsideration for rating of impairment(s)
M21-1MR	III, IV, 2, Section B	Revision of Decisions	
Department of Defense Instructions and Manual			
DODI 1332.38		Physical Disability Evaluation	Determination of military member is unfit for duty
DODI 1332.39		Application of the Veterans Administration Schedule for Rating Disabilities	Determination of military member is unfit for duty
DODM 1332.18 Vol 2		Disability Evaluatioin System (DES) Manual: Integrated Disability Evaluation System (IDES)	Procedure for IDES for individuals going through MEB
Federal Public Law			
Pubic Law 106-475		Veterans Claims Assistance Act of 2000	
38 United States Code (U.S.C.)			
38 U.S.C.	5108		Information and understanding on new and material evidence for claim
38 U.S.C. Title 5	8301	Uniform Retirement Date	Effective date of retirement being on the 1st of the month
38 U.S.C. Title 10	Chapter 61 Section 1214	Right to Full and Fair Hearing	Member of the armed forces may not separate or retire for physical disability w/o fair hearing

43

Social Security Disability Law			
20 CFR	404.1509	How Long the Impairment Must Last	Impairment must have lasted or must be EXPECTED to last for CONTINUOUS period of at LEAST 12 months
20 CFR	404.1520(d)	Evaluation of Disability in General	Impairment meets the duration requirement regardless of education, age, and work experience
20 CFR	404.1525(a)	Listing of Impairments in Appendix 1	Purpose of the Listing of Impairments
20 CFR	Appendix 1, Subpart "P"	Listing of Impairments	

Various VA Forms and Applications in PDF Format

Order Military Records

- SF 180 - Request Pertaining to Military Records (used to obtain DD 214 discharge records)

Intent to File to Establish an Effective Date

- VA Form 21-0966 - Intent to File a Claim

Application Forms

- VA Form 21-526EZ - Veteran's Application for Disability Compensation & Related Benefits
- VA Form 21p-530 - Application for Burial Benefits
- VA Form 10-0103 - HISA Grant Application
- VA Form 10-10EZ - Application for Health Care
- VA Form 21p-527EZ - Veteran's Application for Pension
- VA Form 21p-534EZ - Surviving Spouse or Child's Application for Survivor's Pension, Dependency andIndemnity Compensation (DIC), and/or Accrued Benefits

VA Pension and **Survivor's Pension** are sometimes called the Aid and Attendance Benefit. When applying, the claimant should supply VAwith a certified copy of the veteran's original military discharge. VA will also want to see a copy of a marriage certificate and/ or death certificate when applicable. If there are ongoing care expenses (e.g. home care or assisted living), VA will require VA Form 21-2680 and proof the claimant is paying for and receiving care. Supply VA with statements of from the care provider and invoices marked paid.

Supporting Forms

- VA Form 21-0969 - Income and Assets Statement
- VBA Form 21-22a - Appointment of Individual as Claimant's Representative
- VBA Form 21-2680 - Examination for Housebound Status or Permanent need for Regular Aid andAttendance (Completed by Claimant's Physician)
- VBA Form 21-4142 - Consent To Release Medical Information to the VA
- VBA Form 4138 - Statement In Support Of Claim
- VBA Form 21-0845 - Authorization to Disclose Personal Information
- Care Provider Report (Completed by Claimant's Care Provider)
- VBA Form 21-0779 - Request for Nursing Home Information

Supplemental Information Forms

- VA Form 21-526b - Change in Existing Compensation
- VA Form 21-8049 - Request for Details of Expenses
- VA Form 21p-8416 - Medical Expense Report
- VA Form 21-0516 - EVR Veteran with No Children
- VA Form 21-0517 - EVR Veteran with Children
- VA Form 21-0518 - EVR Surviving Spouse with No Children

Decision Review Forms

- VA Form 20-0995 - Supplemental Claim
- VA Form 20-0996 - Request for Higher-Level Review
- VA Form 10182 - Request for Board Appeal

Veteran Resource List

Organization Name	Website	Services provided	Special Comments
Colorado Outward Bound School	www.outwardbound.org	Veteran's trips	
Challenge Aspen-CAMO program	www.challengeaspen.org	Veteran's trips	
Vet Tix	www.vettix.org	Free tickets or with minimal cost	
Wounded Warrior Family Support	www.woundedwarriorsfamilysupport.org	Family trips	
Military Warriors Support Foundation	militarywarriors.org	homes, job assistance, financial planning	
National Military Family Association	www.militaryfamily.org	Scholarships, Children's camp	Purple Heart
Help Our Wounded	www.helpourwounded.org	phone cards, education, financial assistance	
Take Flight Farms	www.takeflightfarms.org	Equine Therapy	Omaha, NE
Wounded Warrior Project	www.woundedwarriorproject.org	Multiple services	
Warrior Beach Retreat	www.warriorbeachretreat.com	Couple's Retreat	Provide own transportation
Coalition to Salute America's Heroes	saluteheroes.org	Emergency Financial Aid	
VFW	www.vfw.org	Assistance/Support	
Operation First Response	www.operationfirstresponse.org	financial assitance, quilts, backpacks	Active duty and veteran
American Red Cross	www.redcross.org	Family Support	
VFW Foundation	www.vfwfoundation.org	financial assitance, support, phone cards	
VFW Un-Met Needs	www.unmetneeds.com	Financial assistance	
American Legion	www.legion.org	Multiple services	
Operation Homefront	www.operationhomefront.net	Financial, Food, Repairs	
Our Military Kids	www.ourmilitarykids.org	Grants for sports, tutoring, fine arts for children	Reserves, Guard, Active, Vets
National Association of American Veterans	www.naavets.org	VA claim, Finiacial resources, Caregiver Resources	
Hope for the Warriors	www.hopeforthewarriors.org	Trips/activities, Family support, scholarships	
Armed Forces Foundation	www.armedforcesfoundation.org	Family/financial assistance, Education	Vets must have been separated less than 18 months. Active duty
Air Force Aid Society	www.afas.org	Emergency Financial Aid, Education Grants	Air Force Only
Navy-Marine Corps Relief Society	www.nmcrs.org	Financial Assistance, Loans, Disaster Aid	Marine and Sailors only
Army Emergency Relief	www.aerhq.org	Financial Aid, Scholarships, Loans	Active duty, retired, widows
Renewal Coalition	www.renewalcoalition.org	Family Retreat in Florida	
Veterans Airlift Command	www.veteransairlift.org	Travel for wounded Vets	
Air Compassion for Veterans	www.aircompassionforveterans.org	Travel for wounded Vets	
Ohio Military Injury Relief Fund	jfs.ohio.gov/veterans	one time grant	Ohio Veterans
Luke's Wings	www.lukeswings.org	Travel for wounded Vets	
Homes for Our Troops	www.hfotusa.org	Homes	VA Special adaptive housing grant eligible
Operation Second Chance	www.operationsecondchance.org	Trips for Vets/Couples	
Green Beret Foundation	www.greenberetfoundation.org	Assistance/Support	Special Forces
Hero Miles	www.fisherhouse.org	Travel for wounded Vets	
Yellow Ribbon Reintegration Program	www.yellowribbon.mil	Resource assistance	Reservists/National Guard
Heroes Night Out	www.heroesnightout.org	Resource assistance	
The Moonlight Fund	www.moonlightfund.org	Financial, Education	Burn Victims
Soldier's Angels	www.soldiersangels.org	Multiple services	
All Seas Travel	www.allseastravel.com	Military Discount	
Operation Family Fund	www.operationfamilyfund.org	Financial assistance	OEF/OIF
Healing Heroes Network	www.healingheroes.org	Medical help, tablets	
Reserve Aid	www.reserveaid.org	Financial assistance	Reservists/National Guard
Impact A Hero	www.impactplayer.org	Financial assistance, track chairs	OEF/OIF
Fallen Patriot Fund	www.fallenpatriotfund.org	financial assistance	
United States Welcome Home Foundation	www.uswelcomehome.org	Retreats, education	
Rebuild Hope	www.rebuildhope.org	Financial Assistance	OEF/OIF
Project Veteran Aid	www.projectveteranaid.com	Assistance with VA benefits for aid and attendance	
Vets 4 Veterans	www.vets4veterans.com	Resource assistance	
National Veterans Service Fund	www.nvsf.org	Financial assistance	
USA Cares	www.usacares.org	Financial, job assistance	
PenDen Foundation	www.pentagonfoundation.org	Financial Assistance, planning	
Coast Guard Mutual Assistance	www.cgmahq.org	Interest Free Loans, financial planning	Coast Guard
Veteran Love	www.veteranlove.com	Homeless assistance	Miami, FL
Freedom Alliance	www.freedomalliance.org	Multiple services	
Lone Survivor Foundation	www.lonesurvivorfoundation.org	Retreats, education	
Operation Sacred Trust	www.411veterans.com	Homeless assistance	South Florida
Operation Ward 57	www.operationward57.org	Financial, other support	
Team River Runner	www.teamriverrunner.org	Kayaking	
Joint Services Support	www.jointservicessupport.org	Multiple services	Guard, Reserve
Build A Sign	www.buildasign.com/troops	Free Welcome home signs	
National Veterans Healing and Wellness Center	www.veteranswellnessandhealing.org	Couple's Retreat	PTSD Vets
Project Sanctuary	www.projectsanctuary.us	Family Retreat	
Challenge America	www.challengeamerica.com	Resource assistance	
F7 group	www.f7group.com	Multiple services	Female Veterans
Military Assistance Mission	www.azmam.org	Financial Assistance	Arizona Active, Veterans
Samitartan's Purse-Operation Heal our Patriots	www.samaritanspurse.org	Couple's Retreat	Biblical Based
When war comes home don't retreat	www.whenwarcomeshomeretreats.com	Multiple services	Female Veterans
Quality of life foundation	www.qolfoundation.org	multiple services	

| Wounded Warriors Family Support | www.wwfs.org | Family retreats | OIF/OEF |